Wakefield Press

In the Air of an Afternoon Almost Past

South Australia's own Peter Goers is a reformed social irritant. Since 1971 he has worked as actor, director, designer, critic, academic and entertainer on two continents. He began writing for the *Advertiser* in 1985 and has contributed a weekly opinion column in the *Sunday Mail* since 1991. Peter Goers has won eleven awards as presenter, since 2003, of the *Evening Show* on ABC Radio Adelaide, across South Australia and into the Silver City of Broken Hill, and in 2013 he was honoured with the Medal of the Order of Australia (OAM) for services to the arts, community and public broadcasting.

By the same author

Maddening, Self-indulgent Crap – a memoir

Send in the Clouds – a book of paintings

In the Air of an Afternoon Almost Past

A MEMOIR OF LOSS

PETER GOERS

Wakefield
Press

Wakefield Press
16 Rose Street
Mile End
South Australia 5031
www.wakefieldpress.com.au

First published 2023

Copyright © Peter Goers, 2023

All rights reserved. This book is copyright. Apart from
any fair dealing for the purposes of private study, research,
criticism or review, as permitted under the Copyright Act,
no part may be reproduced without written permission.
Enquiries should be addressed to the publisher.

Cover designed by Stacey Zass
Edited by Julia Beaven, Wakefield Press
Typeset by Michael Deves, Wakefield Press
Printed in Australia by Pegasus Media & Logistics

ISBN 978 1 74305 994 4

A catalogue record for this
book is available from the
National Library of Australia

Wakefield Press thanks
Coriole Vineyards for
continued support

Most of all for my sister Jenny who keeps the flame,

and in memory of our grandmothers, Ellie and Mae, who lost their only children,

and for Robert Cusenza, in friendship.

CONTENTS

CONTENTS

There is a house in New Orleans
They call the Rising Sun
And it's been the ruin of many a poor boy
And God I know I'm one

Traditional and The Animals

To lose one parent may be regarded as a misfortune.
To lose two looks like carelessness.

Oscar Wilde, *The Importance of Being Earnest*

The ship is called Independence. *Soon Father appears at the*
rail. Fit and flush, he stands with his hand raised as the ship
steams away, quickly disappearing into the fog. Edwin stays
until Father has vanished. He's left with such a strange feeling,
as if he's forgotten something he should have remembered,
but he doesn't know what it is. This feeling will last the rest
of his life.

Karen Joy Fowler, *Booth*

this thing: a without which
I cannot name.
Without which is my life.

Solmaz Sharif

... these long rainy afternoons in New Orleans when an hour
isn't just an hour but a little piece of eternity dropped in your
hands – and who knows what to do with it?

Tennessee Williams, *A Streetcar Named Desire*

... the disconcerting discovery of how silent destiny is, when,
suddenly, it explodes

Alessandro Baricco, *Ocean Sea*

To move at all in suburban Australia was epochal; people lived
in the same house for sixty years. Often one of the children took
it over, and kept up the same hydrangeas.

Sumner Locke Elliott, *Fairyland*

These events, foretold, are of forty years ago. They were a surreal blur then and remain so. A fever dream that was tragically real. Even with the clarity of time, there is only distance. And the need to understand. I suppose it is a long overdue, long goodbye.

CHAPTER 1

Carelessness

It begins with whom? It begins with bells. Tolling for whom?

The telephone was ringing and ringing and ringing. An incessant annoyance at 11 am on Saturday 10 July 1982. I was a bit hungover. Normally, I'd have woken at the crack of noon and sought the soothing balm and panacea of Mersyndol washed down with creaming soda and black coffee. The breakfast of champions.

The night before, my production of John Whiting's play *The Devils* for the University of Adelaide Theatre Guild had played its second night at the Little Theatre. Whatever is good about a production will be at its best on opening night; whatever isn't may improve. Second nights are often a letdown. The company can be tired, and it realises the real work is only starting.

The Devils concerns a convent of nuns in 17th century France. The nuns fall in love with a glamorous priest and feign devil possession to get his attention. It's a big play with a possession scene in Act Two wherein semi-clad nuns cavort, masturbate with crucifixes, scream and are raped.

The second night had been oddly troubled. Professor Graham Nerlich, actor, president of the Theatre Guild and philosopher, had been taking the tickets at the door. When we reconciled the ticket butts we realised, to our horror, that four punters had presented tickets to the Footlights revue *Have You Checked The Children*, playing at Union Hall across the Barr Smith Lawns on that same night. The BASS tickets all looked the same, hence Nerlich's easy mistake.

So we had four audience members in the wrong theatre at the wrong show. They were expecting undergraduate shenanigans, not the saturnalia of religio-psycho-drama. When Anna Pike entered the stage playing the hunchbacked mother superior, flagellating her hump with rosary beads, four audience members hooted with laughter. Naturally, this distressed Anna and the entire cast. The laughter continued throughout the first act.

At the first interval, Graham Nerlich and I rushed into the theatre and explained to the fun-loving four that they were not at a Footlights revue and their inappropriate laughter was killing the show. They explained that the moment the show had started they'd realised their mistake and since they were going to see both shows they decided to stay put. We realised to our growing horror that it was another four people, legitimately at our show, who were laughing. I don't recall, did we caution them or eject them? Whichever way, the laughter stopped. For this relief much thanks.

After the show we'd have gone somewhere, probably

Don Giovanni's in Rundle Street, to eat and drink. I'd have drunk too much and driven home.

And I was now being woken by the bloody phone, which I answered belatedly and begrudgingly.

It was my beloved maternal grandmother Ellen Myrtle Dunstone, who was 85 and lived in a neat unit a half-a-dozen streets away. I loved her so much. We often called her Ellie but in more serious moments, Nanna. She said with concern, 'Peter, there's been an aeroplane crash in America and it corresponds with your Mum and Dad's itinerary.'

Somewhere deep inside my soul, I knew they were dead. Somewhere, in an even deeper part of my soul, I hoped, silently prayed, willed the universe, that they weren't dead. I also knew I had to be strong for Ellie. I said, reassuringly, 'Oh, Nanna. Thousands of planes come and go in America. It can't be theirs ...'

She replied with mustered composure, 'The accident was in New Orleans and they were leaving there on that day.' She asked me to come to her. I agreed. I hastily dressed and drove my dilapidated VW Beetle to Ellie's house.

Ellie was dressed, corseted and concerned. She showed me the itinerary and, sure enough, Mum and Dad were due to be on Flight 759 departing New Orleans at 4.09 pm on Friday 9 July for Las Vegas. They were at an hotel in New Orleans and due at an hotel in Vegas. We listened to the radio news. It gave no flight number.

Sitting at the phone in the bedroom I began five hours of

frantic phone calls. I rang Pan Am Airlines in New Orleans, Las Vegas, Melbourne and Sydney. I was told constantly no details could be given but my contact details were assiduously taken. I rang the hotel they were due to leave in New Orleans. They had checked out. I rang the hotel they were due at in Las Vegas. They had not checked in.

Ellie made tea and coffee. She sat in her Sanderson linen recliner. Waiting. I was trying to reassure her against diminishing hope.

I suppose I knew they were dead. I suppose she did, too. This bitter, horrible knowledge was wrapped in a thin cocoon of hope.

I then did something extraordinary. With great presence of mind, great focus, using the telephone book and Ellie's teledex, I compiled a list of everyone I would need to call should the worst be confirmed – my sister Jenny, at work as a nurse; Warren Jarrett, my parents' lawyer; my parents' executor Brian Hammond; accountant Andrew Cleland; a few of my friends; Ellie's brother (Uncle Clem) and her nephew Brian and his wife Alison – to come and be with Ellie.

At 4 pm the phone rang. I was sitting with Ellie. It was someone with a kindly, serious voice from Pan Am in New York. They told me my full name and asked me to repeat it. They asked if I was the son of Brian Desmond Goers, aged fifty-two, and Margaret Leonore Goers, aged fifty. Shakily, I said, 'Yes.' They then informed me that my parents had died in a plane crash. I was not looking at Ellie. After a pause, I was then told I must travel to New Orleans the next day and they would call me back with the arrangements. That was it.

'Oh, Nanna, they're gone ...'

Nanna already knew. She took a great intake of breath. I leant by her chair and held her tighter than I'd ever held anyone and that old Baptist of profound faith, her rock of ages, and her poor Christian grandson started to recite the 23rd Psalm.

She had lost her only child, her daughter.

> *The Lord is my shepherd, I shall not want.*
> *He maketh me to lie down in green pastures: he leadeth me beside still waters.*
> *He restoreth my soul: he leadeth me in the paths of righteousness for His name's sake.*
> *Yea, though I walk through the valley of the shadow of death, I will fear no evil: for thou art with me; thy rod and thy staff they comfort me.*

Mumbling now, *my cup runneth over ... Surely goodness ... and mercy ... all the days of my life ... for ever ...*

And then Ellie wept. Deep, deep tears as she held my hand. I have never before or since known such tears.

The phone rang again and she rose and, numbly, automatically, made a cup of tea.

It was a different Pan Am person, who again checked my

details and told me, that as next of kin, I must immediately travel to New Orleans to identify the bodies. Did I have a passport? No, I'd never left Australia. I'd be leaving at 6 am to fly to Melbourne where I'd be taken to the American Consulate and issued with an emergency passport, thence to New Orleans, via Honolulu and Dallas or Houston.

I think I called my sister, Jenny, who had been waiting to hear from us since 9.30 that morning. She had denied the possibility of the worst and gone to work, as usual, as a theatre sister at the Queen Elizabeth Hospital. I rang Ellie's rellies. I rang my father's friend Brian Hammond who told me I was also a co-executor of the estate. I rang my friends, Chris Butler, Teresa Howie, Greg Scudds, others, and I told them not to tell *The Devils* company until after the show that night. I rang my contact in Maitland on the Yorke Peninsula where I was directing *The Sentimental Bloke*, and I rang Michael Pope and asked him to replace me.

Uncle Clem and Aunty Myra arrived to comfort Ellie. Jenny arrived, enraged by grief and incomprehension. She later went to our family home although she was by then living elsewhere with a doctor and returned to be with him that night.

Then I realised that my paternal grandmother, Mae, knew nothing. She did not listen to the radio, except late at night and she rarely watched TV.

I rang her great friend Nell Jenkins. Aunty Nell lived nearby on Torrens Road and I asked her to meet me at Mae's house. She had visited Mae every single Friday afternoon for as long as anyone could remember. Shocked, Nell met me at Mae's and, strangely, Mae was completely unsurprised that Nell and I would walk into her house after dark on a Saturday night with no warning.

Then I had to do the hardest thing I've ever had to do. I had to tell her that her only child, her son, had died. Been killed. She cried short, quiet tears. It was the only time I ever saw her cry. I left her with Aunty Nell and I called the neighbour, Barbara Window (always called Mrs Window) who was very caring towards Mae. Mrs Window was the best Christian I've ever known. I left them to numbness, silence and cups of tea poured from an old aluminium teapot into slightly chipped pastel-coloured everyday cups and saucers.

I had not smoked for two years, mainly to appease my mother. I went to a deli and bought cigarettes and I've not stopped smoking since. I failed my promise.

And, I had failed my parents by not saying goodbye. I'd been very busy, living in the next street in Woodville. I knew they were going to the US to attend a photographic conference in Las Vegas but I didn't know until after they'd left that they'd gone. I had not said goodbye, nor wished them well, and I had no clear memory of the last time I saw these beloved parents living 350 metres away.

I had not said goodbye.

CHAPTER 2

'Hello, I must be going ...'

Who are these people? These dead people. My paternal grandfather Julius Wilhelm Goers (known as Jos to all but those at the Woodville Bowling Club who called him Joe) was Barossa German. He left there after a family division in the 1920s and came to Woodville where he worked on the assembly line at Holden for forty-seven years, and he never had a day off through illness. He had never been to hospital, apart from visiting others.

When Jos was eighty-eight, he was sitting with Mae on the front verandah late afternoon/early evening. He'd finished watering his beautiful old roses lining the low Cyclone wire fence – Christian Dior, Mr Lincoln, Peace and Violet Carson –and the tough buffalo grass lawn. There was mist in the air and crickets chirruping. He said to Mae, 'It's getting a bit chilly. I'm going inside for a cardigan.' Twenty minutes later, wondering where he was, Mae went inside to find that he had put on his cardie, laid on the bed and died. In perfect peace. It was, as they say, 'a good death', and Jos deserved that. He died the year before his son died. He was a lovely, quiet, considerate soul.

My paternal grandmother, the wonderfully named Mary Mae Buggins, was of Famine Irish descent and a tailoress from Perth. Everyone from Perth is perverse and Mae was the most perverse person I ever knew. She was born and bred working class. She swam, played tennis and rode a bike. She was agnostic (they used the term Calithumpian), generous, unambitious, indifferent, funny, frustrating, tough and hard to love. How she and Jos met is lost to me now but they built a Californian bungalow with a red polished-concrete front verandah at 4 Angus Street, Woodville South, behind the Connor Estate, Silveracre, which became the Queen Elizabeth Hospital. The Connors, I swear, were a family of dwarfs, who owned this property replete with wheatfields and market gardens. Jos and Mae lived in that house for nearly seventy years. They were homebodies. Mae went back to Perth a few times and they went to Coobowie once and didn't much like it.

My father, Brian Desmond Goers, born 1929, was an only child. Both my parents were only children. We used to say that their parents had sex once and didn't like it. Brian was highly active for the next fifty-three years. He ran around Woodville. He scarred his face falling onto the edge of a galvanised-iron fence. And he channelled that energy into playing lots of sport, including baseball, basketball and gymnastics at the YMCA.

His first job was on the assembly line at Philips at Hendon. Sometime later, he began work as a commercial traveller for automotive parts companies including Bosch. At one point, he ran a servo at Seacliff. It failed. In the manner of many men of his generation he was a hobbyist. He was a rifle shooter and won the Queen's Shoot (which isn't as funny as it sounds), a bush carpenter, a brickie (in those days if you wanted a shed, you built it), a boatie and a fisherman. He started to make Super 8 home movies, then joined a movie-making club and made lots of short films – comedies, pensive observational films, travelogues – and he turned this skill into a unique and increasingly lucrative business filming weddings (particularly Italian and Greek). He cut a hole in the wall between the hallway and the dining room in order to project movies on a screen in the sunroom of our family house. Later, he built a projection room, a tiny cinema seating twenty people, behind the garage where he would premiere the wedding movies for the nuptial couple and their (often extensive) families. Later, he segued into stills photography, portraits, passports and weddings. Finally, he had found his greatest talent, popularity and some prosperity.

Brian was clownish, annoying, funny, unaffectionate, perverse, prudish, a hard worker, a show-off, a good father, a likeable man. He was either 'on' or 'off'. He rarely drank alcohol and he smoked heavily. He loved movies and taught me how to love them. He and I could discuss our beloved Marx Brothers, Charles Laughton and the work of cinematographer James Wong Howe et al, but not a lot else.

I felt he never really understood me; we loved each other at a remove. I felt I could never please him. I had some six part-time jobs between the ages of twelve and seventeen, including delivering the Messenger Press and selling the Saturday *News* at the Woodville Oval. I worked at John Martins, for an injured courier and for my old man carrying equipment and cleaning long power cords from the wedding movies. Still, he always said to me, 'You couldn't work in an iron lung.' He never, ever hugged me. Men of that generation didn't show physical affection. Sadly.

My maternal grandfather, John Dunstone, known as Jack, was of Irish descent and was raised in a row cottage in Martini Street, Exeter. Mysteriously, his father was found fully dressed and drowned on Semaphore Beach and he was tasked, unenviably, with identifying his body. He worked as a clerk at Elders at the Port, before and after World War I. He served in France, was gassed and died younger than he ought. He was a life member of the Port Adelaide Football Club, where he played for some years as an unspectacular defender. He always said that the only injury he sustained was the day he ran out of the players' race and a woman stabbed him in the buttock with a hatpin. If only today's oft-injured footballers were that fortunate.

I remember little of Jack. He died when I was about ten and we were told that Grandpa had 'gone away'. Similarly my maternal grandmother Ellen Myrtle Dunstone, nee Megaw, would warn us (like a spoilsport suburban Sybil) against swimming at Port Elliot's Horseshoe Bay because 'people had been taken'. Taken where? Ay, there's the rub.

My best memory of Jack is of him driving Ellie, Jenny and me to Victor Harbor for a holiday in a ye olde guesthouse. Jack and Ellie had honeymooned, in common with many nuptial couples, at the Crown Hotel in Victor Harbor. Jack drove us in his Austin Major and we groaned up the old Willunga Hill Road, praying mercifully that the car wouldn't boil because if a car was going to boil it would do so on that infamous and perilous climb. We stopped at the crest of the hill with great relief, and Ellie unpacked a lavish morning tea replete with sandwiches, cakes and milky tea dispensed from an old thermos with greaseproof paper around the stopper as extra insurance. In the manner of his generation, Jack was always hatted outside. But he never wore a hat inside. Oddly, after he'd died a woman he'd worked with at Elders wrote to Ellie to tell her that she and Jack had had a long affair. She enclosed a photograph of the two of them in fond embrace. Ellie showed my mother and said, 'We will never speak of this again.' And they never did. He seemed like the least likely man to indulge thus, but those kinds of men often are the adulterers.

Of all these grandparents, I was closest to Ellie. I loved her very much. We were similar people. We belonged together. We were born sixty years and two days apart, she in 1896. Ellie was raised on a small farm at Stockport near Tarlee where she learned to cook, sew and became a fine watercolour artist. Girls of that era learned the gentle arts. She did not see the sea until she was ten. She stood with her parents at Kirkaldy, near Grange, and burst into tears at her first sight of the gelid, swelling, inimical mass before her, the great green/blue unknown she had only imagined.

I think of that Edwardian girl in her picture hat, so looking forward to seeing the sea, and crying shocked tears at its impact. Ellie remained suspicious of the sea all her life; she also had a fear of thunder. When it happened, she'd go into another room to hide her fear, in the hope she would not transfer the fear to her daughter. She did not, however, hide her morbid, devastating fear of snakes from me and, to this day, I remain terrified of snakes and all reptiles. My mother had a fear of birds which, unlike her own mother's fear of thunder, she successfully transferred to my sister. There are always fears, rational and irrational. What about fear of flying?

Ellie's sister, Vera, married Albert Reed, the feed and grain merchant of Tarlee, and later her brother, Clem, came to town with the family when they left the farm. They lived at Torrensville and Ellie went to work in the shoe department of the Myer Emporium. She was very proud of her working life and could be critical of her contemporary housewives who had (this was said with a knowing sigh), 'never worked'. How Ellie met Jack is lost to memory but they married in the late twenties and my mother was born in 1932, when Ellie was thirty-six, old for a first-time mother in those days.

Ellie couldn't drive or swim but she was a great cook and she loved her food. She set her table thrice daily (table cloth, napkin rings, cruet, etc.) and ate three meals a day whether on her own or with others. She was emotionally and physically robust. A big-boned countrywoman. She loved a far horizon. Her Baptist faith was solid and vital but it was *personally* profound, not annoying or proselytising. She was an amusing, determined, active, caring, diligent and loving mother and grandmother.

My mother, Margaret Leonore Dunstone, was born in 1932 and raised at Helen Street, Pennington. Ellie and Jack moved to Ledger Road, Beverley, after Jack retired to be closer to my parents, who were four streets and a reserve away in Glenrowan Road, Woodville South.

Margaret learned to tap dance because every little girl wanted to be Shirley Temple in the 1930s, and Jack decorated her bike for Empire Day. She was a bright, sporty girl who eventually played women's basketball (later called netball) for the state, and was well remembered at Pennington Primary and Woodville High. She was gauche but a nice girl who became a nice woman. She was raised nicely. One of the sadnesses of my life is knowing that my mother was regarded by her teachers as bright and a candidate for teachers' college but she wasn't bright enough to win a Commonwealth Scholarship (which were very few) and her parents could not afford to send her. Instead she became a secretary and a job was provided at her father's firm, Elders.

My mother was a loving woman, bright, cheery, sensitive, capable, unambitious. She denied herself to further my sister and me. She was a lousy cook. Everything she dished up was either grey or ice cream. Because she loathed cooking she never taught Jenny and me to cook. Both the grandmothers, living very close, were glorious and frequent cooks. We were certainly never hungry.

My parents met at the Glengarry Tennis Club and were married in October 1955. I was born on 28 July 1956. They honeymooned at Warnambool where I was conceived. A honeymoon baby. They built an L-shaped, freestone-fronted, modest, two-bedroom 'Gloria Soame' on a narrow but deep block at 18a Glenrowan Road, Woodville South, around the corner from Mae and Jos and near Ellie and Jack. The Queen Elizabeth Hospital loomed behind the house. My sister, Jennifer Ann, was born in 1959.

The decades prior to the cataclysm were of contentment. Jenny and I were raised with love, the most valuable gift children can be given. We were close to our grandparents and neighbours. When it was no longer seemly for Jenny and me to share a room, a back bedroom for me and a sunroom were added to the house. We went to the Adelaide Miethke Kindergarten (where Mae occasionally played the piano), Woodville Primary and Findon High. Caravan holidays were at Port Elliot and Port Vincent and we took road trips to the Kelly Country and Canberra. We attended the popular and venerable Woodville Methodist Church and went, more eagerly, to Sunday school. My father rarely came to church, and his attendances were desultory and begrudging. Fair enough, it was often boring.

Lawns were never mown or cars washed or rooms vacuumed or washing hung on Sundays (the Sabbath) or Good Fridays. Dad would work in the shed on these days with the door closed. Our lives seemed to be governed by a great stricture of suburbia: What The Neighbours Might Think.

A payday treat was a brick of Amscol ice cream. Neapolitan. I remember the first TV being installed in the lounge room – a Kriesler black-and-white set. We'd watch TV together as a family, the Sunday night movie especially, and Dad would go to Mickan's Deli on Findon Road and buy a family-size block of Cadbury chocolate for us to enjoy sitting on the green vinyl lounge suite watching the telly. We had one painting. It was in the lounge room next to the teak china cabinet and it was a sylvan landscape of gum trees and creek by the German immigrant water colourist Charles Frydrych, who sold his work door-to-door. I think my mother felt more sorry for him than appreciative of his lovely art but I loved that picture.

My parents slept in twin beds. We owned a champagne-coloured Kingswood Holden. We had a teak buffet in the dining room and my mother coveted the much better teak buffet owned by our neighbour, Mrs Edna Ortner. My parents almost never entertained except for Christmas lunch, when we were joined by grandparents and Auntie Ethel Grosvenor, a friend of Ellie's ('who had no one else'). There were financial stresses, but we managed. I can only recall one barney between my parents. Our biggest trouble was kikuyu in the lawns. Lawns were sacred.

In 1971 my mother exhorted me to study harder so I could win the Commonwealth Scholarship she was denied and thus be the first member of our family to go to university. She was also concerned that, if I didn't go to uni, I could be conscripted to fight in Vietnam. My mother worked as a highly regarded secretary of the Preparatory School of St Peter's College. She said she'd get another job in order to pay for me to go to uni. Then, in 1972, Australia changed. The Whitlam Government was elected and Australia withdrew from Vietnam and university education became free.

I was a theatrical without knowing anything about the theatre. At age ten I decided to produce, direct and star in the trial scene from the dramatisation of *The Wind In The Willows*. My mother typed out the script for my classmates on Gestetner stencils and ran off the copies. It was a hit and I was suddenly the Orson Welles of Woodville Primary School. I later saw a lot of theatre thanks to our neighbours, the Ortners, who took me, while my father took their son Richard fishing and to sporting fixtures. Later I appeared in a proper play thanks to my charismatic Grade 7 teacher, Mick Rivers, and in third year high school I wowed 'em at the Woodville Town Hall as The Artful Dodger. My life was thus charted. My parents who'd once been to the theatre (to see *The Pajama Game* at the Theatre Royal when my mother was pregnant with me) were perplexed by my theatrical ambitions and neither encouraging nor discouraging.

Jenny was sporty like our parents and played netball for South Australia. Mum also coached the netball team at the church. I was briefly a Sunday school teacher until I was sacked for dramatising the parables with my charges. Sunday school concerts were a highlight, with the entire student body sitting on scaffold bleachers at the front of the church, and occasionally there were little plays performed by the impossibly glamorous first family of the Woodville Methodist Church, the Noblets. The patriarch, Don Noblet, was a noted actor at the Adelaide Repertory and his children also performed. One day they arrived at church to take their regular front pew and Helen and Peter Noblet had blonded hair because they were starring in *The Sound Of Music* at Her Majesty's Theatre. I almost swooned with the glamour and excitement of this.

I went to Flinders University to study drama and stayed there for eight years, eventually abandoning a Masters degree (which was a great disappointment to my mother). My whole reason for being was working in the theatre – and teaching swimming to pay for it. My life was spent just lurching from show to show. Living my art. This came at the cost of my Masters. I was too busy and too distracted working in the theatre to study, although I eternally promised, in the words of the eponymous Charley's Aunt, Lord Fancourt Babberley: 'I've lost an awful lot of time over these theatricals. But next term I mean to work.' But I didn't. Jenny studied nursing at the Children's Hospital and became a highly respected theatre sister, a profession she still follows.

By 1980, Dad had achieved success as a stills photographer of weddings and portraits, my mother was working with him, as was a lovely neighbour and family friend, Marie Edwards.

Dad bought a house in the next street, 41 Glengarry Street, for two reasons. Firstly, he wanted to get rid of me from the house (highly understandable) and, secondly, he wanted to create a huge wisteria arch in the backyard of the quarter-acre block under which he could photograph brides. I moved all my books and my op shop clothes in many wheelbarrow trips.

So, in three generations, my family had moved two streets. We were not adventurous people. Woodville suited us, a halfway place, old/new stolid suburbia. We knew people. People like us.

We knew of Peg and Alf Cathro who had owned 41 Glengarry Street, Woodville South. We didn't actually know them because they were Catholics and these were the sad, strange days of the divide between Catholics and Protestants. We were told that Catholics answered directly to the Pope. When I was about fifteen, I said at the tea table, 'I met a Catholic today,' and everyone was amazed. Ellie had a good friend who was a Catholic and she'd say, 'Kath is an awfully nice person ... for a Catholic.'

I had delivered the *Weekly Times* Messenger Press newspaper to the Cathros from a sagging cardboard box octopus-strapped to the back of my deadly treadly. They lived opposite the house where Chips, the neighbourhood dog, a beautiful, loving, roaming kelpie-cross, lived. When Wittgenstein said, 'A dog has no knowledge of next Wednesday,' he had not encountered Chips. The dog would wait for me every Tuesday in his front yard and then follow me on my round. Alas, every time I threw a paper (rolled and rubber-banded by the indefatigable Mae before I came home from school, her hands black with newsprint), Chips would fetch it. This became an actual and existential newspaper deliverer's crisis and I'd have to put dear Chips behind his back fence.

Peg and Alf Cathro had lived in their modest bungalow their whole long married life. Alf expired in the afternoon sun in the dinette. He was 'gathered' or 'promoted to glory'. Peg expired three days later at the letterbox, clutching sympathy cards she'd retrieved, cards probably from his old work, and from the bowling club, the Rechabites, and the little girl down the road for whom he'd made a doll's house.

The Cathros had not been blessed with issue but the Cathro had kith. The 'Kithro'. The house was sold to my father, I moved in, and Peg and Alf were benign ghosts. They'd kept their little house 'just so', as Ellie said when she inspected it. Alf's very neat and orderly shed was just as 'just so' as the neat-as-a-new-pin home.

Our family spent two Christmases at my house and, on the Christmas of 1981, I had an appalling, inane, ridiculous argument with my mother. We argued very rarely but this argument went on for days, and in my rancour and her tears it ruined her last Christmas on earth and my Christmases ever after. It was all my stupid, stubborn, bombastic, immature fault.

And so, on the fateful, frightful, stricken night, the cold, cold winter's night on which I was orphaned, in which my parents' bodies lay mangled and lifeless a long, long way from Woodville, I returned home.

And I had not said goodbye.

CHAPTER 3

'Leaving on a jet plane
Don't know when I'll be back again
Oh, babe, I hate to go ...'

By now I was chain smoking. I stopped at Mum and Dad's house where I saw my still-enraged sister in the driveway. She had been at Marie Edwards' house, next door but one. Family friend Marie worked part time for my father. I tried to hold my sister. 'They've gone, Jenny, they've really gone ...' Her tears were the rags of her soul. She would not be held, she would not be comforted. I told her I had to go to New Orleans to identify the bodies and told her to look after the grandmothers. She left in her car. Our family house was now a sort of shell, like that left by a dead sea creature. The love and the lives it held were now broken, different, empty. Somehow, it was no longer our house. It could no longer offer harbour and comfort.

The house I rented from my father one street away (though my mother more often than not slipped me the modest rent for me to give him) was dark, cold and suddenly unwelcoming.

Kind, good friends I'd called earlier came. We shared incomprehensible numbness. Shock. Muted tears. Although, had I cried? No. I hadn't time to cry. I was involved. Moving on towards America. Moving towards death. I had to pack. I had to leave. I had to fly in planes just like the ones that had killed my parents. My courage came from the need to do this big final thing for my parents. Identify them. Claim them. Bring them home. One last time.

Show folk Teresa Howie, Chris Butler and Craig Elliott came first, and Gregg Scudds (who had a small role in *The Devils* and was my assistant director) and the actor and fatherly good bloke Bill James, and maybe others from the play came after it had finished. I was drinking brandy but was not drunk. Craig Elliott brought Valium, the first of that drug I'd ever taken. That softer fog was welcome. Soothing. I moved determinedly, as though I were underwater.

July 1982 was experiencing a particularly cold winter, now very much of discontent. Helped by my friends, Chris and Teresa, I was packing winter clothes – my op shop Harris tweed jackets, overcoats, corduroy trousers ... My friends, themselves shocked by the tragedy, were trying to tell me through the fog of Valiumed, brandied grief and determination that I was going to a hot, humid summer in New Orleans, and not to wear and take winter clobber. I didn't, wouldn't, couldn't listen. I was assembling a plastic bag full of a pharmacopeia of prescription and patent drugs. This became a lifelong habit. Chris, especially, warned me against this, to no avail. A hypochondriac is never dissuaded. People made coffee, tea, perhaps people drank brandy with me ... People came and went, saying things, being sorry, feeling abject, expressing useful, useless pity. No one ate. We wouldn't have lit a mallee-root fire for fear of extinguishing it before leaving at 4.30 am for the airport, so we were warmed by a two-bar – three-bar? – radiator. I felt the sort of cold that couldn't be relieved. A deathly cold ...

At some point, the Pan Am people had called telling me I'd be catching the 6 am flight from Adelaide to Melbourne, thence I'd be taken to the American consulate where I'd be met by a person from the Australian Department of Foreign Affairs who would issue me with a passport and stick my photo in it and I'd be issued with an emergency American visa. During this long night's journey into day, I'd contacted a photographer friend of my father's who had met me at my father's studio behind the family house and taken a Polaroid passport photo. I looked drawn, exhausted, wired. I looked 'other'.

Numb. Focused. Distrait. Focused. Empty. Focused. I had a mission. I had to travel across the world to identify the bodies of my parents. This was my focus. We moved out of the cold house into the pre-dawn of Woodville, of home. The cold was such that inside a house seems colder than outside.

Teresa and Chris took me to the airport with my ragtag luggage. We were met by my father's friend, Brian Hammond, who worked for Telecom and before that the Postmaster General. He had supplied us years before with what were then illegal and very handy phone extensions.

Brian and I were co-executors of my parents' estate. He was kind, a good man in shock. But focused. He presented me with a will to sign. My will. This left everything to my sister Jenny. It was witnessed by someone. I didn't know he was doing this but it was sensible. I might have been killed, too.

I learned later that my friends, Teresa and Chris, had gone to the newsagency at the airport and turned over the copies of the *Sunday Mail* so I couldn't see the picture of my dead parents on the front page.

We moved through the airport as though underwater. As though swimming towards a shark, full of fear. I now had to get on a plane. My parents had just been killed in one and I had to get on another. Focus. Friends. Nodding. Hugging. Fear itself, willing me forward and holding me back. On. The wide-eyed, red-eye, bull's-eye flight.

Now I'm in the plane. In a moving, full metal coffin. I don't want to move. I must be moved. Be propelled via death to help identify the bodies. Later, I realised the airline had blocked several rows. Left them empty. Of course ... it would be ghastly and unfair to other passengers to sit next to or even in the proximity of a person who has just lost loved ones in another plane and will be fearful, and heaven forfend they shared their fear and grief and lamentations.

In those days we called flight attendants 'hosties'. An older, very sympathetic hostie sat next to me. She said nothing. She didn't have to. She was just there. She was a kind, reassuring, compassionate presence. She held my hand as the plane taxied down the long long long runway, and squeezed my hand as we took off in that miraculous, hopeful moment of defiance of gravity and sense and breath. She helped me. I'm very grateful to her and I suspect she was put on to that flight for me. We talked a little, not about death, not about horror, but of little things. Maybe another hostie served coffee I can't remember drinking. My hostie was my comfort. Thanks, ma'am. Thanks.

Then I'm at Tullamarine in Melbourne. The Pan Am people express sorrow but no apology. Considerate. Taciturn. Formal. What can they say? I'm on a mission to leave Australia. I'm driven through dank, depressing suburbs. Was it raining? Probably. Lightly. Purposefully. I'm tired and wired. I'm trying to concentrate but I'm being led. I think I was taken into Melbourne to an office of the Department of Foreign Affairs, a Victorian Victorian stone building where my awful passport photograph was stuck in my passport, which, the day before, I had no idea I'd be getting. My needs are now immediate. Was I taken to the American Consulate for my visa, or was the visa already in the passport? Or was some servant of the United States of America and his/her stamp with us? I don't recall. Nor did I care. I was a human parcel.

I'm flown to Sydney in a much bigger plane. Another 'hostie' sits next to me. This time we are in first class but there are still seats blocked around me. I'm deplaned in Sydney and sitting in another departure lounge. I can see flags at half-mast. I'm smoking incessantly in those halcyon days when you could smoke as you flew.

When was I aware of the full cataclysm? When did I know that 153 people had been killed and the plane had landed on a suburb and killed eight people, including six children playing on the streets after school. When did I comprehend that there was shared grief and loss? I don't know. Quickly, then slowly? I was consumed with my own unimaginable personalised loss and unable, unwilling, to comprehend the mass of it.

And I'm flying. On a mission. To identify bodies. Did I sleep, finally? Did I eat or drink? Was there a moment of peace or consolation? There was just the noise of engines, harsh lights, soft lights, a blanket, the day/night, while reading the same two sentences in a book in a big plane travelling to another time, the day before I left. I was empty, exhausted, beyond thought and suddenly beyond fear of flying.

Perhaps it was at this time I began to feel that life was useless, that life could be snuffed out instantly. These were good people. What was the point of living?

Honolulu, Hawaii. As I stepped on to American soil for the first time in my life, a cirumstantial tourist, my bag strap broke. It was a camel-coloured webbing shoulder bag from an army disposal store; a cheap bag often sported by students. Someone helped me restore the strap and pick up all that had escaped. It was a manifestation of what I was feeling – eviscerated.

I kept seeing my parents' faces. I kept thinking I saw them walking along. The fantasy of believing they are really alive (that it hasn't really happened) and all this is a stupid, shocking mistake lasts for years.

Hawaii seemed bright and hot from the airport. We had stopped to drop off and pick up. In those days long-haul flights did this and ongoing passengers were allowed to deplane and stretch their legs. I just plopped numbly, waiting. Eventually I was back in the plane and for the first time there was no hostie sitting next to me for takeoff. I was back in first class. I never feel I deserve first class. Mae's exhortation rings in my head: 'You know why we're in second class? Because there's no third class.' But I didn't care, here and now. My only use is that I'm being sent to do a final service to my parents by identifying their dead bodies. Their cadavers. My only sense is that I'm flying in a plane like the one my parents were killed in and I'm at the mercy of the airline that killed my parents. This is no way to fly.

A pleasant, elegant, middle-aged man was sitting next to me. He was a movie producer. He was considerate and happy to talk. He was a diversion on the journey from Honolulu to Los Angeles. I must have told the Sydney/LA hostie I was a movie buff and they must have asked this chap who was a regular flyer to help me, and he did. I was grateful.

Los Angeles. City of Angels. Fallen angels. Horror. Pan Am staff take me through immigration and we bypass customs. My luggage is being sent to New Orleans via Houston. Just like me. It's now late afternoon and I'm told my next flight (to Houston) leaves, incredibly, at 2 am. I'm led like a blind dog to an hotel. The Pan Am man leaves me after I'm checked in and told to order anything I wish and to meet someone from Pan Am in the lobby at 1 am, and a bellboy takes me to my room. I tip an Australian note. I have no American currency. I order brandy. They sent cognac. I drink it and don't get drunk. I'd so like to be drunk. I turn on the TV in this dark, cold (I'm always cold) room. The movie *Little Murders* is showing and I scoff at the irony. It's a funny black comedy by Jules Feiffer and I'd seen the play at the Scott Theatre, years before. I'm not laughing but staring. And sitting. Drinking. Time passes.

I finally start to cry for the first time. A wave of exhausted, lonely, panicky, jagging grief hits. I moan. I'm scared. I have no one. I can barely remember where I am. After a while, how long I don't know ... hours ... I realise I cannot move. I cannot walk. I'm stuck in an anonymous depersonalised limbo.

I call downstairs and I'm weeping on the phone and I say I can't move and they must call the Pan Am people. Sometime later – how long? – another Pan Am person and a bellboy arrive. The latter lets them in and I tell them I can't move. They haul me out of the chair, gather up my bag with the broken strap and practically carry me down to the lobby. I regain some motivation and the Pan Am person walks me to a terminal and puts me at a table in a cafe in sight of the check in counter for my 2 am flight. He leaves me. I'm hours early for the flight. I'm in an empty cafe in an empty terminal in an empty airport. Empty but for my thoughts, but even they are vacant. Sense seems to have left me.

Time passes. I don't know what time it is. My watch is still on South Australian time. I start to obsess about this watch. It's a modest silver Seiko watch I was given for my twelfth birthday. It was a rite of passage. I was taken to town to Wendt's Jewellers in Rundle Street by my mum and Nanna Ellie and told, within reasonable prices, to chose a timepiece. We'd have had lunch at the John Martin's Buttery or the Myer Polo Lounge. Balfours pasties and chips, scones, cakes.

This was the watch later stolen by John Lahr, the greatest theatre critic in the world and son of the great comedian Bert Lahr, who played the Cowardly Lion in *The Wizard Of Oz* and, later, Estragon, in the American premiere of *Waiting For Godot*. I believe Lahr fils's biography of Lahr père is still the finest biography of an actor. John Lahr came to the Adelaide Festival in 1976 and gave a lecture at the State Administration Centre Theatrette. He came on to the stage and stood behind the lectern, saying he'd left his watch in his hotel room and could he borrow one? I was in the front row with my ears back and hastily proffered my twelfth birthday Seiko, proudly passing it to the great man across the footlights. He placed it on the lectern, spoke brilliantly and bemoaned the lack of Australian theatre in this Australian festival. At the end of his talk, he acknowledged applause, pocketed my watch and walked off stage and out of my life forever. I raced backstage but he'd vamoosed.

I rang the Festival office and was happily able to retrieve the watch at which I was now staring, a million miles from home in a cold, deserted airport, the second hand the only thing moving. And the time was out of joint.

After a while, I became panicked again, started to cry, was embarrassed, then didn't care and, once again, I was stuck, immobile, rigid. Time passed. Finally I saw a Pan Am hostie arrive at the check-in counter. Immobile, I called the waiter and asked him to summon her. He did. She came. She and the waiter helped me to a seat near the counter and eventually she and the waiter supported me on to the plane. It was a very old Pan Am plane. I was plonked into a first class seat and, extraordinarily, there was only one other passenger, a middle-aged woman in economy.

There was only one hostie on the flight and she did not offer to sit with me. We took off, rattling, me in silent, stony, fucking terror. Then it got worse. I asked the hostie if the only other passenger would sit with me and I was told that told that was not allowed. The hostie was churlish and disappeared during the four-hour flight. No food or drink was offered. I chain-smoked. Where had the cigarettes come from? I can't remember. Maybe someone from Pan Am had supplied a duty-free carton.

Subsequently, I realised that I was on a ghost flight, a flight put on for me. Who the other passenger was I had no idea. She ignored me. Perhaps she was as scared as I was. Then it got really scary. We flew into a storm and the plane bucketed violently in the turbulence. I looked out the window to see multiple lightning strikes. Was I going to die? Was this the lightning that was going to actually strike twice? Was Pan Am trying to kill me as well?

At least this current nightmare within a nightmare, this present crisis, jarred me out of my weird, numb stupor into real, adrenalin-wired panic. I clung on. The turbulence was so rockingly severe I couldn't get out of my seat. I breathed deeply. Fear focuses one. There was a copy of the *Los Angeles Times* magazine, the rest of the newspaper, full of news of the plane crash, had been removed for my benefit, but there was a profile of the actor George C. Scott who was opening on Broadway in a revival of Noël Coward's *Present Laughter*. To distract myself, I spent hours memorising the first paragraphs of the profile. Whispering it like a catechism. The night passed.

Exhausted, red-eyed and strangely energised I was deplaned

into a terminal in Houston ... to more half-mast flags, another Pan Am staff member and ubiquitous sorrowful remarks but no apology. I moved breakfast around a plate, drank black coffee, then was escorted to another, busier plane, sat in a blocked row unassisted by a hostie.

To arrive, finally, in New Orleans.

CHAPTER 4

Chucked

And another airport. The final airport in more ways than one. I'm met by another Pan Am operative. The pattern is set. I will never meet the same Pan Am people more than once. This gives them plausible deniability. The game has started, the legal quagmire just beginning to suck me down.

This is Chuck. Of course, his name had to be Chuck. This also describes what I want to do. Quarterback Chuck from Central Casting is tall, blonde and boxy and speaks with a polite Southern drawl. He is formal and firm.

I'm standing at the arrivals gate with Chuck when a woman thrusts herself at me. She's tiny and well dressed, with sandy-red coiffed hair – and very pushy. She grabs my hand and tells me her name is Verna Weisgerber and she's friends with Trevor Buggins, a distant cousin of mine in Perth. She's been waiting to meet me. To help me.

Chuck moves me away. Chuck won't tell her where I'm staying. Chuck moves me on. I'm confused. We collect my luggage. We walk through the terminal.

Chuck warns me not to talk to anyone. Why?

Outside, I'm assailed by a wet blanket of incredible heat and astonishing, crippling humidity. I have never experienced this before. My knees buckle with the pressure of the crushing, hot damp.

Chuck puts me in a mercifully air-conditioned taxi and tells the driver to take me to the Sheraton Airport Hotel at Metarie. He pays him. He leaves. Farewell, Chuck.

During the five-minute drive, the obese, cigar-chewing, Southern cracker taxi driver says, 'Y'awl.' I scream with laughter. The driver is confused. I thought 'y'awl' was something only caricatured Dixie hillbillies said. Surely no one actually says that. I thought it was the equivalent of Australians saying, 'Gidday, cobber,' or English bobbies saying, 'Hello, hello.' I was so wrong. 'Y'awl' is ubiquitous in the South. It is a conversational glottal stop. I had much to learn.

At the hotel, another Pan Am operative meets me, checks me into the hotel, gets the key and takes me to my room, pushing the luggage cart himself. I learn later that this room faces the crash site, several kilometres and many stands of trees away.

The room is nice enough, with two double beds, a TV, a telephone and a Gideon Bible. New Pan Am guy tells me that other Pan Am representatives will contact me soon and I'm not to leave my room. Why? I'm told they'll tell me.

Minutes later, there's a knock on the door and another Pan Am person, a man, asks me to follow him. I'm taken to another room where I meet several Pan Am lawyers; suited, middle-aged lawyers.

They are very formal. I'm not offered a drink. They express guarded regret. One of them passes me a piece of paper and says, forcefully, that it's in my best interests to sign this paper for compensation and I'll be able to leave New Orleans and return home immediately.

I look at the piece of paper. I am being offered $10,000 in compensation for the death of two parents killed in the prime of their lives in the care of Pan American Airlines.

I'm a kid, in a foreign land and not in my right mind. I fiercely decline, glaring at the assembled company.

'I'm here to identify the remains of my dead parents. When, where and how do I do that?'

'That is not possible or necessary.'

'So why am I here?'

'To discuss compensation and provide medical information to help with the identification of—' he looks at his list '—Brian Desmond Goers and Margaret Leonore Goers.'

'I've been advised not to sign anything.'

'That's unfortunate.'

I'm being made to feel both defensive and guilty. I'm not told anything about the process of identification. I'm now asked questions about my parents' health and medical conditions. I'm told that I must provide details of the names and contact information for their doctors and dentists. I'm to do this expressly as this will aid identification.

Naturally, I tell them all I know, mainly in response to questions being peppered at me.

'Did your parents smoke?'

'My father, yes.'

'How much?'

'A packet a day.'

'Did either of your parents wear glasses?'

'Yes, my father always, my mother to watch TV.' I volunteered that my mother had varicose veins.

More and more questions, mostly answered in the negative. I gave them names: Dr Lyall, Dr John Moore, the dentist Graham Mount.

Then they told me in stern terms that unscrupulous ambulance-chasing lawyers had come from all over America to New Orleans touting for the business of the next of kin and that, by law, American lawyers take thirty per cent of any compensation and it was their job to keep me from these lawyers. There were other next-of-kin families staying in this hotel and they forbade me to speak with them. I was to stay in my room so I could be available to Pan American Airlines at any time. I would be required to meet with Pan Am representatives daily. This was very important and I was to compile and gather any information pertaining to my parents' medical and dental records I could. I must call home and ask the doctors and dentists for all these records to be sent immediately. Only this would aid positive identification.

They then presented me with another piece of paper offering me $20,000 compensation, which I declined.

At this I was told I was foolish and not to expect any compensation at all. Only then did they finally ask me if I needed anything.

I asked if I could see the crash site.

'That is impossible. It's dangerous and it's controlled by many different government agencies and emergency services. Impossible.'

I was conscious that the entire wardrobe of tweedy winter clothes that I had brought from a cold Antipodean winter were absurdly inappropriate and I explained this and asked to go to a shop to buy summer clothes; I also asked to see a doctor. I wanted sleeping pills. They told me they would arrange this. I was escorted back to my room, paranoid, scared, fucking exhausted and worried about the problems of identification. I had no idea that identification of charred bodies in an exploded plane is purely forensic, but I was learning.

I saw people in the corridor. Bereaved people. I so wanted to talk to them. I so needed to talk with them. The Pan Am dude led me away.

Despite the air-con, I sweltered as I unpacked in my heavy clothes. Soon, yet another suited Pan Am man arrived. He gave me $200 US and said he would take me to see a doctor and to JC Penney's to buy clothes. Off we went in another taxi, the dude taciturn. We arrived at a nearby strip of shops and, while my minder sat in the waiting room, I was taken in to see a doctor. His name was Cerrato. He had obviously been told of my predicament and on greeting me said in a Southern drawl I was becoming attuned to, 'Why shit, son!' He then asked, 'How can I help y'awl?' I told him I had customary trouble sleeping and I had only slept fitfully for days. He prescribed Seconal and wished me well. 'Our fine city is so sorry for y'awl, son.' We then had the prescription filled at Kare Drugs in Kenner. The druggist's name was Schexnaydre, I know this because I still have the Seconal bottle, long empty, a bonny barbiturate indeed.

I was then taken to a nearby JC Penney and escorted in by my minder. I bought two pairs of chinos, cream and grey and two collared cotton shirts.

Back in the room I started to watch the blanket coverage of the clean up of an airline disaster, a few kilometres away.

The plane had taken off at 4.09 pm, hit wind shear at the end of the runway, turned violently, hit trees and landed on the suburb of Kenner – landed on and razed many houses, its full fuel tank exploding into a cataclysmic fireball. The plane had only ever gained an altitude of between 90 and 150 feet.

I could envisage distraught people, ruined houses being bulldozed, bits of the plane, fire hoses, emergency services workers and dead bodies, some in body bags.

Welcome to New Orleans. Welcome to hell.

CHAPTER 5

'A little piece of eternity ...'

I began my routine of calling home late at night to suit the time difference and to check on the grieving grandmothers, Jenny and others. Jenny reported in great distress that plain-clothes police had come to the family home and finger printed everything, leaving a film of black dust throughout the house. This was to aid the identification of the bodies. Marie Edwards, lovely neighbour and my father's employee in the photographic studio, was being helped by family friend and photographer John Atkins. They were arranging photographers to take over bookings for weddings and portraits and were delivering ordered photos. Jenny told me that she'd had a crank call late at night asking if she knew where her parents were. She replied with the candour typical of her, 'Yes, they're dead in someone's backyard in New Orleans.'

I requested that she contact our parents' doctors and dentists.

The Seconal was a blessing. A chemical oblivion. I slept in the embrace of the very welcome Sandman, long and completely. But when I woke, I was still in a strange hotel room in New Orleans. I was sequestered in a velvet prison, scared, alone, waiting – and warned. I was both wanting to watch and not wanting to watch the blanket TV coverage of the cataclysm.

I was summoned to another meeting with Pan Am lawyers. They were different lawyers in a different star chamber. They repeated the offer of $10,000 compensation. Outraged, I told them I had refused that yesterday and there was a counter offer of $20,000. They denied all knowledge of that.

'We see you are interested in money,' they drawled.

'I'm only interested in my parents being identified.'

'Ah, yes, have you requested medical and dental information?'

I said I had.

They then commented that I had travelled to New Orleans alone. I was outraged now. 'There was never an offer to bring someone else!'

'Is there anyone you'd like to be with you?'

My best friend in the world, the actor Robert Cusenza, was in Europe on a delayed honeymoon with his wife Rosa. They agreed to bring him to New Orleans. Sometime later, on my instruction, Rob was contacted in Zurich by my friend Teresa Howie in Adelaide and hastily agreed to fly to me. Pan Am had made all the arrangements and he left immediately. He'd had no idea of the tragedy.

Another day passed. It was sunny. Then it wasn't. It rained. I could see a freeway and trees, beyond which were the remains of my parents and so many others. There was the TV and there was room service. This was my first experience of that. I came to realise that the two best words in the world are 'room service' – 'It's benign' are good, too. Among the worst words in the world are 'salt damp' and 'white ants'. 'Your parents are dead' are shocking words.

The Pan Am people in New Orleans had contacted a Pan Am operative in Adelaide in his office on King William Street. He contacted Jenny to confirm the names of the doctors and dentist. Since only a next of kin can request such files, or, presumably, the police or a coroner, Jenny asked them urgently for the files.

The highly renowned dentist Dr Graham Mount had prepared my parents' files and charts as soon as he heard about the accident and gave them to my sister. We later learned that Australia's pre-eminent forensic odontologist, Dr Kenneth Brown, was at the University of Adelaide. He also had the charts from Dr Mount and worked with the New Orleans forensic odontologists. Dental records are crucial in disaster identification.

My father's longtime GP, Dr John Moore, provided records but, extraordinarily, my mother's GP, Dr Allen Lyall, declined. My sister went to his surgery on Woodville Road and begged for the files and burst into tears of rage when Dr Lyall declined.

Later, through Pan Am and presumably under the authority of the New Orleans coroner, a uniformed policeman came to the family house and took the files to the airport.

Back in New Orleans, I was isolated, confused and despairing. I felt a great urgency to identify the bodies and the wait was a torment. I was alone in a strange place, grieving in the Hotel Kafka, with a TV showing multiple deaths and the ubiquitous highly patterned synthetic bedspreads common to hotels and motels the world over.

Late at night I talked to Warren Jarrett, our lawyer, and others at home. I'd been offered no help from anyone in all of America. I found the number for the nearest Australian Consulate, in Houston, and I called, only to be told that it was a trade mission and they couldn't help me. It was me against Pan Am, and against the time it was taking to identify the remains.

I was also a prisoner.

Then things improved.

Unbeknown to me the New Orleans newspaper, the venerable *Times Picayune*, had published a photo of me in a huge series of spreadsheets with photos of many nexts of kin who had come from all over America and the world. I didn't see this for some days, as Pan American continued to deny me the newspaper.

In hindsight, I wonder why I just didn't go down to the lobby? But I was young, inexperienced and traumatised, not only by grief but by Pan Am, who had instilled this absurd fear in me.

In the *Times Picayune* was a photo of me, probably from the *Advertiser*, accompanied by a brief description, which said I worked in theatre in Adelaide, Australia. By then, many in New Orleans had realised that many nexts of kin were put up at the Sheraton Airport Hotel and the feisty Verna Weisgerber called me. She was highly sympathetic and caring. At last, a friend had been found. Or found me.

I met Verna and her husband Leo – vice-president of a small insurance company – in the lobby. She was a pretty sixty-year-old Dresden doll, beautifully coiffed and dressed. Leo was considerate and kind; she was a worrier. She gave me Minties she'd brought back from her last trip to Perth. The Minties seemed sacramental to Verna. She'd met Leo during WWII in Perth when he was on shore leave from the US Navy and they married after the war. She came to New Orleans as a war bride.

Verna and Leo filled me in with all they knew about the accident and we kept in touch. I was grateful for their concern.

Then Rob arrived. I have never been so pleased to see someone. Pan Am had flown him to me first class. He was my first-class friend. We had worked together many times in the theatre, he was a wonderful actor and a fine friend. We were soul mates. We were the same age and had grown into friendship through the theatre. Our relationship has been crucial to my creative development. He was my muse. Everything I achieved as a director in this period was because of Rob Cusenza, and generally with him. Rob was and is a person blessed with charm, comedy, courage and chutzpah. As a student at Christian Brothers College he auditioned for the school's entry into the annual Catholic Schools' One-Act Play Competition and failed to win a role. He rang the organisers and asked if it was possible to have two entries from the same school. It was, so he directed and starred in a production of Chekhov's *The Proposal* and won. A born gambler, Rob is the second youngest of a strong Italian family. He was the person I always needed most in my life, especially here in New Orleans. A rock.

His presence was immensely reassuring and I suppose I talked at him for hours as we sat in that strange room above a freeway, in view of trees, close to a cataclysm, in one room in an hotel full of other rooms full of other people's grief.

The morning after he arrived he looked at me oddly and told me that I must take the Seconal while in bed, ready for sleep. Apparently, I'd taken it the night before and fallen asleep while sitting on the side of the bed removing a shoe. Rob had had to undress me and put me to bed. Lesson learned.

Rob stayed with me for two days. We were taken to a meeting with yet another cast of Pan Am lawyers, escorted into a waiting car by a Pan Am operative. The meetings had moved from the Sheraton to a nondescript motel nearby.

Once again, there was no update on the identification and they demanded all medical information again. When I told them I had already supplied this information, they said, not to us. After the meeting canny Rob told me that he thought I was being recorded. The following day at yet another pointless meeting in the same motel room, Rob asked to use the bathroom and he was told it was out of order and he was taken to the bathroom in the neighbouring room. Bingo.

We were paranoid, with good cause.

The phone rang in the hotel room and a man introduced himself as secretary to the Archbishop of New Orleans. He asked whether I'd take a call from him. A little confounded, I acceded. While waiting for the Archbishop to be connected, I tried to think of how you address same. I was a reformed Methodist and this was my first Prince of the Church. It came to me, probably from a play ...

'Is that Peter Goers of Australia?'

'Yes, Your Grace.'

'This is a very difficult time for you and your family and I'm calling to ask you if there's anything I can do for you?'

'Thank you, Your Grace, but I'm not a Catholic ...'

'I didn't ask you that ... how can I help you? I'd like you to meet Father Earl La Rose of the Kenner Parish. He was one of the first people on the site after the accident and he's worked tirelessly ever since.'

'Thank you.' I then voiced what was a great concern. 'I'd

like to go to see the crash site. Pan Am won't allow me to go. Can you please help?'

'What?' quoth His Grace, outraged. 'They won't allow you to go? I'll call you back shortly.'

Ten minutes later the Archbishop called again and said with triumph, 'Pan Am is sending a car immediately to take you to the crash site. It'll be downstairs waiting for you.'

'What did you do?' I asked him, incredulously.

'Well,' said His Grace, 'I rang my contact at Pan American and told them unless they sent a car for you forthwith, my next calls would be to NBC, CBS, ABC and the *Times Picayune*, all of which would be highly interested in a young man from Australia who's lost both his parents in a Pan Am crash and who is denied seeing the crash site.'

It was a lesson in the media. I thanked the Archbishop and I will always honour his kindness, compassion and media savvy.

Rob and I hastened to a waiting big black car. Just a few kilometres away we were confronted by heat and dust and the smoke from pyres of bodies. This was nearly five days after the accident and you could still smell gas, airline fuel and burned bodies in the miasma of humidity. Whole houses had been razed by the plane, others burned in the fireball alongside those tarpaulined and partially demolished. Oddly, some houses in the path of the plane were completely unharmed. Body parts were still being collected and laid into body bags. There was the noise of bulldozers and many emergency workers from all manner of agencies. People were exhausted. We were taken to a large tent where the workers were fed and watered. We met many of them, thanked them. We met the extraordinary Father Earl La Rose, in shirtsleeves and dog collar. He had kind, loving, eyes red with emotional trauma. We saw bits of the plane, bits of wing at odd angles, bits of fuselage fused to buildings and trees. Everything seemed infused with tired energy and death. And oppressive heat. Heat, heat, wet, fetid heat.

Father La Rose introduced Rob and me to neighbours, first responders, workers, survivors. I felt part of something. For the first time, the death of my parents was no longer abstract but a very real part of an enormous disaster in which I could now share.

That included the smell of charred human remains. Forty years later I can still recall that horrific smell amid the dust and heat and magnolias.

CHAPTER 6

'When magnolias last in the dooryard bloom'd'

Sweet, sickly, pungent magnolias were everywhere. It was late in their season and vast, monumental trees with dark green leaves were drooping with huge, blowsy, waxen, white blooms, which flower and shine, glisten in the rain and fold and die within days. They perfume the humid air. But they don't drop. They die on the tree.

The chronology of what happens next is cloudy.

Rob said, 'Why are we sitting in this hotel room? The Pan Am people really don't need you. They are waiting for the information to come from home. You are signing nothing. We're in one of the great cities in the world, a city we've always wanted to visit ... let's go to the French Quarter.'

I agree. Rob has given me courage to defy Pan Am. Fuck them. This was the second day Rob had been with me and his last. We would be tourists.

Verna is horrified that we would go into the French Quarter, which she claimed was dangerous. Rob and I both thought this absurd. Surely this historic, highly touristed precinct is safe?

We arrived in the French Quarter, got out of the taxi and walked across a zebra crossing near Canal Street. Halfway across a woman grabbed my arm and spun me around. Was Verna's warning prescient? Jesus Christ, I'm being mugged! I thought. The woman exclaimed, 'Peter Goers!' It was Leona Gay, Adelaide actress and former TV personality from *Adelaide Tonight* with Lionel Williams, among other shows. I'd seen her as Olive in *Summer Of The Seventeenth Doll* at the Q Theatre in 1973, and she is still the best Olive I ever saw. The only Olive who got the howl at the end of the play right ... the howl of a Greek tragedienne. And here she was 15,449 kilometres from home howling *my* name in the middle of a street.

Leona was on her honeymoon with the legendary Bill Davies, ex copper, radio star and former manager of NWS 9 in its halcyon years. They said they'd seen my name in the paper and wondered how they could find me. And, by happenstance, they had. I agreed to meet them at their hotel after Rob had gone.

Both Rob and I love the plays of Tennessee Williams. The first play I directed Rob in was *The Glass Menagerie* at Way Hall in Pitt Street (next to Her Majesty's Theatre), a production that was subsequently revived at the Q Theatre. Rob was superb as Tom. Our knowledge of and fascination with New Orleans principally came from Williams' masterpiece *A Streetcar Named Desire*. We had watched the film with Vivien Leigh and Marlon Brando many times. It was a theatrical gospel.

And here we were, extraordinarily, in New Orleans.

'They told me to take a streetcar named Desire, and transfer to one called Cemeteries, and ride six blocks and get off at Elysian Fields.'

And: 'those cathedral bells are the only clean things in the Quarter'.

Old buildings, French iron lace, Bourbon Street pulsating with jazz, blues, honky tonk piano, trumpet wails. A small black boy tap dancing in the street for coins calls out, 'Hey, Australia!' He's spotted my RM Williams boots.

Magnolias dripping green and white. Heat. Damp. Sun. The Moon Walk by the cathedral down to the mighty Mississippi, which charges past huge, wide and brown. Paddle streamers.

Tourists, louche locals, mint juleps, beer, cafes, oyster bars, gumbo, Creole, noise, promenading people, spivs, whores, the lost, the found. It's a port in a storm. There are bars open to the street with no doors at all. They never close. The street is all here. People tumble out of buildings on to it. The French Quarter seems like an enormous stage set.

And there are lots of black people. Every second face is ebony. I'm embarrassed to think that all the black faces were shocking to me. Of course, in dear old Adelaide, we didn't see black people. You almost never saw Aboriginal people. More's the pity. They were kept away from cities. I'd sometimes see Aboriginal boys on hot days jumping off the Torrens Weir in to the water as I passed on the train to or from town, and there were some Aboriginal girls in the deaf school attached to Woodville Primary School. They had blank expressions, now attributed to the fact that they were stolen from their families and homes.

Other than them, and seeing Charlie Perkins on the news, and Marcia Hines and Ronne Arnold and a handful of other black entertainers on stage and TV, what did I know of black folk? It was a sad tenor of the times that I'd seen more white people in blackface on TV in *The Black And White Minstrel Show* than actual black people.

Now every second person around me was black.

Because the *Times Picayune* had described me as working in the theatre, every single theatrical and cinema management in New Orleans had contacted me at the hotel and kindly offered me tickets. I will never forget this hospitality and indeed after Rob left I went nightly to sit in theatres and cinemas because I felt safe in the embrace of plush, and what I knew to be true and comforting.

We found the Toulouse Theatre, it was playing the African-American musical *One Mo' Time*. It had been running at this theatre for years. I introduced myself to the manager. He remembered offering me seats so we arranged to return for the show that night. We told him we revered Tennessee Williams and we were told that he was in town at his house in Royal Street, opposite a laundromat he also owned. I had read that his house had no laundry so he'd bought the laundromat nearby and would go there to wash his clothes.

Starstruck, Rob and I rushed around there. The house was on a corner with windows and front door on the street. Nervously, we knocked on the door and it was answered by the prissiest, nelliest young queen I had ever (and have still ever) encountered. The sort of young man who, bless him, can put an 's' in 'banana'.

'Yesssss,' he glowered. We burbled that we were theatricals from Australia and we revered Tennessee Williams and we begged a chance to meet him. The catty catamite looked us up and down and hissed, 'Never heard of him!' and slammed the door in our faces.

We walked around the corner and stood by a shuttered window of the house. Then, as we waited, the shutters parted at a short man's height and dark eyes looked out at us. It was Tennessee Williams. We gasped. We called through the window to no avail and we laughed. It was the first time I'd laughed in nearly a week. I said to Rob, 'See, if you were prettier, we'd have been in there!'

So, I never met the great Tennessee Williams but our eyes met.

We prowled the quarter in the heat and the delightful squalor. It's a place of noisome, jangling joy, a sort of lackadaisical creativity, spicy food and cold drinks, all damped by languor and lassitude. A place worn down, both enervated and energised by heat and time.

We saw and enjoyed *One Mo' Time*, a celebration of black vaudeville with cracker songs which seemed to have come from the very streets we had walked: 'Down In Honky Tonk Town', 'Cake Walkin' Babies From Home', 'C.C. Rider', 'He's Funny That Way', 'Muddy Waters', 'After You've Gone', 'There'll Be A Hot Time In The Old Town Tonight' and, best of all, 'You've Got The Right Key But The Wrong Key Hole'. Despite all this jollity, I fell asleep, perhaps because at last I was comfortable and at home in a theatre.

I told Rob that we could do *Streetcar* now because I understood it. It's about the heat and the noise, anyone can go mad here in this heat. He would play the bête noire Stanley Kowalski. And we did the play the next year. And we both felt the play. It had become part of us.

We left the French Quarter and Rob sadly left the next day to return to his delayed honeymoon in Europe. I was alone, but less alone, and I was so grateful for his love and support 'when magnolias last in the dooryard bloom'd'.

CHAPTER 7

'The kindness of strangers'

I met with Father Earl La Rose, who said grace at lunch at the hotel and told me stories of the noise of a plane diving and dying and the fortitude of those who arrived to help. Of the shock, the shock, of the communal grief and of the baby plucked from the ruins of her house. This gave great, abiding, much-needed hope. Life from death. He was a lovely man.

I met with Verna and Leo Weisgerber and had more Minties, passed to me again as if a sacrament. I went with Verna to a supermarket en route to visiting her house. This little lady drove an enormous American car and, to my amazement, when we arrived at her house in a completely non-threatening *Leave It To Beaver* middle-class American home, she took an enormous pistol out of the glove box and walked with it to the trunk of the enormous car and placed it on the top of her shopping.

Leo and Verna showed me pictures of them with Republican Vice President Spiro Agnew. The highlight of their lives seemed to have been their invitation to a Vice

Presidential Dinner in New Orleans, even though they voted Democrat. It was a lesson in how seriously Americans view their presidents, even veeps.

They also drove me around New Orleans and, at my fervent request, down Desire. It's a very industrial street at the back of the French Quarter – and entirely unexceptional. To my amazement, because it's in or near a black ghetto, Leo locked the car doors with an automatic clunk of real or confected fear. This was my first experience of this kind of security.

At the restaurant in the hotel, Verna pointed behind her and mouthed the words 'black people', referring to the people sitting behind her. That said, she was a funny lady and very considerate of me.

I was getting out and about and I often had the feeling I was being followed.

I went to a flea market in the French Quarter, near the old streetcar named Desire, which is permanently displayed, and I suppose because my picture had been in the paper, it must have got around that I was at the market, or maybe I told a stall holder of my loss, and an old African–American lady came up to me and put a silver bangle in my hand. The bangle is a Victorian design of two hands meeting. She said she wanted me to know how sorry the people of New Orleans were and how much they cared. I wept for the kindness of strangers.

I went to the small New Orleans Civil War Museum and

made a mistake. I was admiring toy Confederate soldiers in the gift shop when I stupidly asked the attending docent if they also had Union soldiers. Outraged she said, 'There are no Yankees here, son!' Oops. I didn't whistle 'Dixie'. Americans have never stopped fighting the Civil War.

I took a bus tour of the ritzy suburb, the Garden District. We saw beautiful ante-bellum houses and grand old trees dripping with Spanish moss. It, and the French Quarter, are redolent of faded romance and spent energy. And the omnipresent heat and humidity. One is constantly drenched in sweat and then chilled in air-conditioning.

There were very few people on this bus excursion and I was befriended by a middle-aged African–American couple on vacation from Chicago. They were thrilled to discover I was Australian and announced that I was the first Australian they'd ever met. They were especially keen to meet one because they owned cable TV and, unusually, watched and loved Australian rules football every Saturday night with their friends. So far so good.

But, they were still confused by some of the rules and were so keen to ask an Australian to clarify them. I had assiduously spent a lifetime avoiding football. I had been exhorted to play a game in second year at Findon High School but I was pulled off by the coach, so to speak, after the first quarter. He had screamed at me, 'You are supposed to run towards the ball, not away from it!' So ended my football career.

I knew nothing about football, except that I detested it. I had attended the odd Sturt game with Rob Cusenza, standing on the flat near the great coach Jack Oatey, but I always seemed to be looking the wrong way. I also went to the Sturt/Norwood Grand Final at Football Park with Rob and his assorted brothers, and since Sturt lost by a point, the brothers Cusenza were practically suicidal on the long way home.

Now a very nice African–American couple were looking to me for guidance. I was so embarrassed. They peppered me with technical questions about the great Australian game. Feeling that I was an unwitting ambassador for my beloved Australia and, not wanting to disappoint, I lied. I made up answers to their questions. They seemed pleased.

I have often pondered those nice folk returning to Chicago and watching Australian rules footy and informing their friends of the definitive rules verified by an Australian. I blanche at their confusion, but I also smile.

The Pan Am meetings became fewer. It was a waiting game for identification. I availed myself of the tickets so generously offered to theatre and movies. I saw the awful movie *Shock Treatment*, a follow-up to *The Rocky Horror Picture Show*. I attended *The Sound Of Music* at a dinner theatre (then very fashionable) at the Beverly Dinner Playhouse, which had been a swanky old illegal casino. A year later, on 7 July 1983, it burned to the ground.

Fire. Water. Stone. Trees. New Orleans.

I took Leona and Bill Davies up on their offer of lunch at

their commodious hotel in the Quarter. They invited me to swim in the hotel pool. Bill was portly and his bathers swam on me, so I went down to the Quarter to buy bathers – or 'trunks'. I found a dusty menswear store and was served by a languid young African–American woman. She showed me the swimming trunks and I chose a pair and took them to her at the counter. She then rang a bell and the owner of the store, a fat fuck cigar-chewing Southern cracker in braces, emerged from the backroom. Only Burl Ives or Ed Begley could've done this man justice. The poor put-upon shop assistant stood aside and the boss rang up the purchase, took my money, made change, closed the till and left without a word. The young woman then put my trunks in a bag and thanked me. I realised, shockingly, that this black worker was not allowed to handle money. Welcome to the South.

Leona, Bill and I took an excursion on the paddle-steamer the *Natchez*, up and down the raging brown 'ol' man river'. I'd never seen a river run so fast. They were very kind to me and, to further divert me, Bill, who'd been a famous 5KA radio announcer prior to taking over Channel 9, pretended to narrate, much as he'd done on air, a royal visit of the Queen Mother.

Her Majesty, the Queen Mother, alights from her car and waves at the adoring crowd. She's greeted by the Lord Mayor, the Right Honourable Robert Porter, and the Lady Mayoress, Mrs Porter, who bow. A dear little girl, Shirlene Saegenschnitter, bows deeply and hands the Queen a beautiful posy of snapdragons. Little Shirlene smiles broadly as Her Majesty and says a few words to her. Her Majesty waves again and the crowd roars and Her Majesty is guided towards the reception line of dignitaries. Her Majesty is wearing a peacock-blue dress of shantung matched with white gloves and shoes and a beautiful hat resembling a hydrangea. The triumph of this much-heralded royal visit continues apace.

We laughed like drains.

More theatre. I was invited to attend the summer stock repertoire at Tulane University; Verna and Leo took me. The first show was Lillian Hellman's *Another Part Of The Forest*, sequel to *The Little Foxes*. Unfortunately, Leo and Verna couldn't find the theatre in the Tulane University campus so I was late. This was the first and, to date, only time I was ever late for the theatre. I was led in by the manager and to my abject horror realised that it was theatre-in-the-round and my seat was on the other side of the stage so I had to squirm cross the stage, between the actors ... excuse I. How embarrassing.

It was an excellent production and a thrill to see a play set in New Orleans, performed in New Orleans. After the show I was introduced to the director and complimented him and asked him how his charges went with the next play in the repertoire, Alan Ayckbourn's then very fashionable play *Bedroom Farce*, since it was an English play requiring English accents. The director was derisory of this enquiry and insisted his actors were completely professional and their English accents were perfect.

The next night I returned, mercifully on time, and was sadly reminded of the near impossibility of playing farce in the round. The American actors' attempts at an English accent were appalling. I heard either no attempt or ridiculous Cockney and other inappropriate, jarring, half-baked accents. American actors (with some notable exceptions) seem unable to master English accents and I pondered that Australian actors do a much better job of American accents.

The 'Nawlens' accent continued to fascinate me, especially the ubiquitous 'y'awl'. At an oyster bar with Rob Cusenza, a waitress taking me to my table managed to use 'y'awl' seven times in one sentence. 'Y'awl are welcome here and y'awl sit over here and y'awl look at the menu while I bring y'awl some ice water and y'awl enjoy the view of the street and y'awl will cool down right here and y'awl enjoy y'selves, y'hear ...'

I was at home in these theatres, welcomed, cosseted, safe and distracted. I'd return to my lonely hotel room and call home and my loved ones wanted to know the progress of the identification. I had no news.

Now I started calling the Pan Am lawyers demanding progress. No news. The wait seemed endless. There seemed to be fewer people in the hotel so I assumed others had had successful identifications of their loved ones' remains and could return home.

It was time for another meeting in an empty hotel room. New lawyers. They'd had at least my father's medical file and the medical information I'd given them about both parents. The lawyers wanted to discuss compensation. I tell them I'm not interested in discussing that, I'm only interested in my parents being identified. They ignore this and continue to talk about compensation.

I'm told that compensation is strictly calculated on life expectancy and loss of earnings. Now all the medical information is used against my healthy, active mother and father, aged fifty and fifty-two, information that had been conned out of me ostensibly and urgently for identification.

'Your mother had varicose veins and she wore glasses, therefore she would've had a heart condition and diabetes and would have been dead at sixty, maybe sixty-five. Your father was a lifelong heavy smoker so he'd have been dead of lung cancer in five years. He also wore glasses and probably had cataracts and diabetes ... Neither of your parents could have expected to earn for more than a few more years ...'

This was horrifying. This was legal hardball. It was ugly. I refused to comment. They then said they preferred to send me home since I had no role in the identification. I repeated that the very reason I was brought to New Orleans was to help in that process. They denied that I was ever told this. Furious, I said I was not leaving until my parents were identified. I walked out of the meeting.

Miraculously, my parents were identified that same day.

I'm convinced news of a positive identification was delayed so that Pan Am could bully me about what they were only ever interested in – compensation.

Finally, I could go home to grieve with family and friends. I could go home to bury my parents. I could go home with my parents. I was asked whether I wanted my parents in caskets or cremated. This is not something I'd thought about. I chose caskets. Later I was told that the remains would be ready the next day and a homeward itinerary was arranged.

I rang home that night and told Jenny, who was greatly relieved. I asked Jenny to start organising a memorial service.

The next day, at the airport, I was anticipating caskets to arrive on the tarmac. Instead I was presented with two very heavy, boxy bronze containers, which I was expected to carry as hand luggage. And I did. I remember nothing of the journey home except lugging my parents through airport terminals to change planes. I was now an economy passenger with no assistance from Pan Am staff.

My parents and I arrived home and I kissed the ground at Adelaide Airport.

The funeral was arranged for 28 July 1982. My twenty-sixth birthday.

CHAPTER 8

'Funerals are pretty compared to deaths'

Says Blanche Du Bois in *Streetcar.*

Pan Am Flight 759, cleared for takeoff, left the ground in a thunderstorm and gained between 90 and 150 feet (between 27 and 46 metres) in altitude when windshear – a microburst of the thunderstorm – forced the plane down. It hit trees and a few seconds later landed in the New Orleans suburb of Kenner, adjacent to the runway. The pilot tried to steer the plane toward a canal. The plane, with a full fuel load, exploded on impact, the fire killing more people than the impact. All 145 passengers and crew and eight people on the ground, including six children, were killed. One-hundred-and-fifty-three people. It was the second-worst accident in America at that time.

In very heavy rain, amid fire and smoke, eviscerated bodies were strewn over the remains of houses, streets and trees. A gas pipe exploded. Some people were burned to death strapped in their seats.

Passengers hailed from twenty-three countries. Julia Ledet lost her parents, and her uncle and aunt. Miami mobster Willie 'The Tile Maker' Dara and his wife were killed. Six-year-old Lisa Baye had ninety-five per cent of her body burned and she died that night. Three hundred members of her family's church stood vigil. Doubtless, there are thousands of stories of the bereaved, as 153 souls are missed in a million different ways on all the days of their lives not lived.

Amid the cataclysmic carnage, amid the putrefaction and heat and smoke, amid the diligence of hundreds of emergency service workers from many different agencies, a baby was found alive in the ruins of a house. Sixteen-month-old Melissa Trahan's mother and four-year-old sister were killed in their house but Melissa's cot overturned and the mattress protected her from the debris. Her discovery and survival proved a great inspiration to those working on this dreadful site, an experience often described as 'like walking though hell'. Melissa Trahan became 'the miracle baby'.

Inevitably there were also stories of people who missed the plane or decided at the last moment not to go to Las Vegas on that flight.

Policeman and part-time Pan Am employee Nick Congemi, was one of the first on the scene and has remained a great support to the people of New Orleans and to the bereaved all round the world. He became Police Commissioner and a nearby police station is named in his honour.

At Our Lady Of Perpetual Help Catholic Church in Kenner there is a memorial bearing the names of all who died. For the fortieth anniversary of the tragedy in 2022, the memorial was fully restored and rededicated by the Governor of New Orleans, and my sister Jenny and her great Louisianan friend, Dr Julia Ledet.

Jenny said:

My brother Peter and I bear the tragic loss of our young parents Brian and Margaret Goers grievously but we are united in grief and loving remembrance with so many other families from New Orleans and all over the world in this community of Kenner, which continues to honour the victims of this terrible tragedy. We are eternally grateful to Father Earl La Rose, late of this church, all the emergency service workers and all the good people of this community. Thanks, also, to those who have cherished this memorial and given it new life and continued presence and honour. We grow together in commemoration and friendship as we reach out to one another across distance and time to share our loss and our lives. And we remember the words of Tennessee Williams from his immortal play set in New Orleans, A Streetcar Named Desire, *'Sometimes there's God so quickly.' Thank you all. Lest we forget.*

Since this tragedy, aviation regulations regarding windshear warnings have become mandatory. Planes sit on runways until the risk of windshear has abated. So lives have been saved from the sacrifice of 153 souls, and for this relief, much thanks.

CHAPTER 9

'Apart from that, Mrs Lincoln, how did you enjoy the play?'

So I was home in my little house and now I had a dog; my mother's dog, a samoyed kelpie, a beautiful white, medium-sized, smiling dog. Snowy The Wonder Dog had been with my sister at our family home but the moment she came to live with me, she started to grieve. She didn't eat for days. She sat by the door waiting for Mum and Dad. It was an awful grief and, like all grief, impossible to relieve. So we grieved together. Only time helped poor Snowy recover and she became one of the most beloved and precious things in my life. Years later I grieved her deeply, indeed and strangely most deeply of all, because Snowy seemed the last part of my parents. Gone.

And Snowy might have saved my life. Weeks after my return, the winter was still cold and Snowy was still waiting for my parents to return. Rob and Rosa Cusenza had returned home and Rob was coming to my place to see me. I lit a big fire in the big open fireplace in the little bungalow in Glengarry Street and waited for Rob, who was very late. I fell asleep near the fire and was woken by Snowy barking and scratching my legs. A mallee log had fallen out of the grate and was burning on a hearthrug of old carpet underlay. I opened the front door, grabbed the burning log in the rug and charged outside with it and, just as I dumped it on the front lawn, Rob arrived and we hosed it off.

Snowy was fine after that. She seemed to understand that she was responsible for me and, indeed, somebody had to be.

I remember little of those weeks after returning from New Orleans. The funeral at the Woodville Uniting Church, formerly Methodist, was large and formal. Jenny and I escorted Ellie and Mae. It was the first time in forty years that Mae had been to church. There were refreshments in the hall. People were kind, considerate and removed from what our little family felt. Nothing fills that void.

At no point during this entire catastrophic experience did Jenny or I ever hear from a single politician, nor was I helped by any public servant from the Department of Foreign Affairs while in America.

I'd seen the last performances of *The Devils* and that show had, as all shows must, gone on. The company was dedicated but also dulled by my grief and my absence. The cast party couldn't have been much fun. I was too sad, too reduced, too numb to get drunk. I hadn't yet realised how to drink through the pain, but that soon came.

I attended the opening night of a musical at the Arts Theatre and, at the party in the upstairs rehearsal room after the show, the veteran critic Harold Tidemann came up to me. In a variation of the enquiry made of the president's widow – 'Apart from that, Mrs Lincoln, how did you enjoy the play?' – Harold asked me, 'How are you, dear, and how did you enjoy America?' Dear old Harold ... I laughed and said, 'Not much.' Not much more to say about all that, really. Then we talked of more important things like show business. It was a healing moment. A bit of perspective.

I went to Maitland to see the production of *The Sentimental Bloke*, which I'd had to abandon and Michael Pope had taken over. He'd done a lovely job and was popular with the company. It was a beaut production of a beaut show. I saw other, many other, shows in Maitland over the years, did shows there and in Minlaton, and became very close to Lois Greenslade, who many of us call The First Lady of the Yorke Peninsula. She's a good Christian woman, stylish, funny, dignified, loving and forthrightly honest. She means a great deal to me because I love her as a friend, and also because she's uncannily like my mother. They are the same age, and the same type of woman. When you lose family members you find others like them. The need for people you once loved and were loved by can be transferred. I found other mothers and fathers and I tried to show them the love and honour I might have shown my parents, had they lived.

In the last forty years, I've watched my contemporaries watch their parents age, become highly dependent, fall over, suffer illness, go to nursing homes, go gaga and die. Some have said to me, 'You don't know how lucky you are not to have had to watch your parents go through this.' And I've replied, 'Well, get fucked ... you're missing the point.'

Ellie coped well in her unit at Woodville for a few more years and we then moved her to the Resthaven nursing home at Malvern, where she lived happily, eating three meals a day until the day in 1992 when she died of a swift heart attack at the age of ninety-five. She never stopped missing her daughter but she lived on in her rock of ages faith and, as ever, made the best of her long life. Her faith is the reason I remain a Christian, a poor, doubting, cynical, non-practising Christian. Nearer my God to thee? Ok?

Mae did it tough. She became more perverse, more eccentric and she slowly went mad. She took in ironing for some years. She became increasingly agoraphobic. She almost never left the house. As her dementia increased, she'd lock herself in the house and lose the key, which is an agoraphobic's dream. She imagined people were stealing from her. She hid things. She still cooked for Jenny and me – especially Cornish pasties and occasional beautiful jelly cakes. She'd sit for hours at the dining-room table staring into space. She eschewed street clothes and lived in a nightie and dressing gown and did not bathe. For years prior to the accident she had slept on an iron cot in the sleep-out at the back of the house which was, at least, near the loo and her expansive laundry, which she called the 'wash house'. She'd listen to Bob Francis on the radio and quote him. She was both lonely and anti-social.

In the late eighties she asked to see me. She said, 'I've never asked you for anything, have I?'

'No, Nanna, you haven't.'

'Well. I'm asking you this ... I want you to promise me that I'll never leave this house, except in a box.' Foolishly, I did promise her that.

She lived on boiled chops and stewed fruit. We arranged Meals on Wheels, which she didn't want, and on the day it was delivered she threw it at the deliverer. Meals on Wheels management rang Jenny to say, 'Sadly, your grandmother is not a good candidate for our service ...'

In the early nineties she'd ring me at Norwood and tell me that someone had stolen her teeth. I'd drive to Woodville, find her missing dentures, settle her and return home. She'd then call again immediately to tell me that someone had stolen her teeth.

Mae was an unwavering Labor Party voter and despite her agoraphobia she insisted on being taken to vote. She loved to vote for the ALP, even in her very safe Labor seat. She declined my offer of securing a postal vote and so I took her to vote, two blocks from her house and where she had last played the piano, at the Adelaide Miethke Kindergarten in Oval Avenue, Woodville South. When we arrived the Electoral Commission had no record of her name and she couldn't vote. She said nothing but it was the second and last time I ever saw her cry. It was as if she were disappearing, ceasing to exist.

Jenny was much more patient than me and she took over

the care of both grandmothers. She was diligent and loving. As soon as I left the country in 1996, Jenny put Mae in a nursing home, Resthaven at Westbourne Park, where she was comfortable and surprisingly genial. I visited her on my return to Adelaide in 1998. She had no idea who I was but seemed happy. And well fed and cared for. She died in 1999. Her house in Angus Street, Woodville South, was bought by singer, director, producer, teacher David Gauci, who was raised near Mae's great friend Aunty Nell Jenkins who, like us, he also loved. The house holds the ghosts of those who never really wanted to leave it ... and rarely did.

Years later, I climbed in a canoe on the Swan River in Perth with Mae's beloved niece and grand-niece Pat and Julie McKnight, and in that rocking, highly unstable vessel we gave her ashes to the water she so loved.

Jenny and I had to clear out our family home and twenty-seven years of our family life. Stuff. The clothes that still smell of the living and everything you touch reminding you of the missing: ramekins, Tupperware, ashtrays, the frypan (of many an egg combo), the bowl of dripping in the fridge, towels, the twin beds, the wedding present mirror, teak nut bowls, the stoneware coffee service, a few books, handkerchiefs, candlewick bedspreads, a chenille dressing gown, old greeting cards in a box covered in wallpaper in the linen press, the Charles Frydrych watercolour ... Did we erase the marks on a door jamb in the kitchen where Jenny's and my height had, yearly, been marked?

Jenny was still full of rage. Grief brings extreme emotions to a raw surface. We fought. We even fought physically and rolled around on the back lawn hitting one another and screaming. Perhaps we thought if we were angry with each other it would help. It didn't.

A man from Perth rang me. Sadly his name is lost, but he and his wife had been aboard the *Natchez* on the Mississippi at New Orleans with Mum and Dad. He recalled how happy they were, and how they told him with pride about Jenny and me. This was lovely and reassuring to hear. Jenny rang him and spoke to him.

Having once been a champion rifle shooter at the Dean Range, our father had given up this hobby and rid himself of all but two guns. The .22 rifle and a beautiful antique shotgun, given to him by great-uncle Albert Reed, were locked in a cupboard in the shed. The .22 was there but the shotgun was never found. We looked everywhere, even in the roof space of the house. It was gone. Dad was extremely careful with guns, as he'd taught me to be when he took me to shoot rabbits on the Yorke Peninsula when we were on holidays at Port Vincent. Once, on a crowded beach, he abused a young spearfisherman walking along the beach with his weapon loaded.

The missing shotgun remains a mystery. He would never have sold it but perhaps he lent it to someone who never owned up and just kept it. I can't imagine him lending the gun to anyone who wasn't honest enough to admit to its loan. We reported it missing to the police and I applied for a licence to own the .22 which, in those days, was absurdly easy. You went to a police station and answered a few multiple-choice questions. Should you climb through a barbed-wire fence or drive with a loaded gun? No. Ok, here's your gun licence. Years later I foolishly lent this rusty rifle to a mad poet. He, and the gun, came to the attention of the police and when they returned it to me, I asked them to destroy my father's last gun.

Life mooched on. Back at the Theatre Guild, Kim Durban was directing *The Tempest* and inexplicably cast me as the 'noble savage', Caliban. That I accepted this role is indicative of my unreliable judgement at this point. It was the greatest piece of miscasting since John Wayne played Genghis Khan in *The Conqueror*. I lasted one rehearsal. But I was soon back directing, acting and designing, soon back in the unreality of the theatre which was life to me. I also secured my first full-time job as Historian at the Performing Arts Collection of South Australia, and worked with actress and curator Jo Peoples and the legendary director Colin Ballantyne, who was the chairman of the collection and a god to me.

The next year, 1983, I directed Tennessee Williams' New Orleans masterpiece, *A Streetcar Named Desire* and the company dedicated the production to the memory of my parents. Show folk are intimate strangers and this gesture was the kindness of intimate strangers.

In 1983 I was rehearsing *The Elephant Man*, with Rob Cusenza playing the title role. Very unusually, we were rehearsing in the foyer of Union Hall, a space we shared with popular public toilets. A man we had never seen before walked in and crossed the foyer to the loo and Rob and I were astonished. It was my father, or a man who looked astonishingly, uncannily like my father. Rob knew my father well. He had filmed Rob and Rosa Cusenza's wedding. We waited, breathlessly, for the man to egress and Rob and I watched him, mouths agape. Is it true we all have a doppelgänger? I do. Recently someone sent me a picture of the German lawyer Albrecht Götz von Olenhusen who, poor bastard, could be my double.

Jenny bought a house in Prospect and Barry Humphries once swam in her pool. I moved across the Port Road to Hughes Street South and an expansive old villa with almost no garden except for a front lawn in which I planted a magnolia tree. Nine years later, when I moved to Norwood, I had still not seen it bloom. Perhaps it has by now.

Our lawyer Warren Jarrett worked on the compensation case. Because the American system allows lawyers to claim one third of the compensation, many American lawyers contacted Warren looking to take the case. One unhinged lawyer even came to Adelaide from America to see Warren and when his services were declined, he inexplicably announced he would take a taxi to Coober Pedy.

We eventually engaged Speiser Krause, a New York firm highly experienced in the field of airline litigation. Warren Jarrett went to New York to work on the case.

As I suspected, I had been followed in New Orleans. The Pan Am lawyers were critical of me, this 'grieving' son, who went to the theatre every night. Also Pan Am attempted to charge us for my airfares, and Rob Cusenza's, and our accommodation. Eventually an offer was made and I asked former Chief Justice John Bray for his opinion. He recommended that Warren and I consult Bruce Lander QC, which we did.

What are two lives worth? Something. Nothing. Money. How much? Strangely, neither I nor Jenny, or even Warren Jarrett, can remember the amount but it was substantial in the 1980s, but it soon went. It was blood money. It bought a few houses and some bad investments and my demands on that money created a huge, ugly rift between Jenny and me that lasted for many years.

These deaths left me, not exactly with a death wish, but the feeling that there was no future. Grief becomes guilt and guilt becomes … fuck it, who cares, my parents died young and I probably will too. And so I did my best to hasten it. Everything but the immediate seemed pointless, and the immediate was the eternal transience of the theatre, show after show after show, and of endless parties and booze.

Alcohol palliates pain, grief, guilt. I had a lot of palliation. Before the tragedy, I was a bad drinker. I would drink too much socially. I could never nurse a drink. I'd drink to get drunk. After the accident I would drink to pass out. I woke on many strange floors in many strange places. I was an embarrassing, messy, loud, showy drunk.

I once fell asleep drunk at the wheel of my car on Port Road at the Rosetta Street traffic lights, where I was woken by the police and told to go home. This was at 3 am and, inexplicably, I was on my way into town. I once dropped a bottle of vodka on the front veranda and mopped it up and drank it from the bucket. There were many such horror stories but I partied hard and people of the night (especially actors and journalists) were happy to party with me. Drinkers love company. Only two people were honest enough to tell me I had a problem, my friends Rob Cusenza and Lois Greenslade, and I salute their honesty. They helped save me.

After one alcohol-induced crisis, I just stopped drinking. It was 10 December 1987, and I've never drunk alcohol since. I was not an alcoholic, I was a binge drinker with no future, trying to forget the horror, the horror ... and, luckily, I never missed alcohol. Teetotalism turned me into the wowser I was raised to be. Funny that.

My sister ran. She ran fast and often. She cycled, swam and she still exercises compulsively to this day. She has tried to outrun the horror ... the emptiness, the loss.

The loss of our parents was much harder on Jenny than it was on me. She felt it more deeply. She was still living with Mum and Dad at the time of their deaths, and she was very close to Mum. She also felt the loss of, especially, her mother when she became a mother of two. She mourns our parents deeply. She also honours them and has returned to

New Orleans many times to attend memorials where she's made firm friends among those, like her, who lost loved ones, and who were scarred by the cataclysm.

Unsurprisingly, I was left with a terrible, morbid fear of flying. I could only fly if I was chemically enhanced – drunk or stoned on Valium. To this day I fear each take-off. Then, in the early nineties, I was in Surfers Paradise writing a story for the *Sunday Mail* and the local photographer invited me to bungee jump. I did. Twice. It was empowering. A few hours later I was sitting on a plane about to take off to bring me back to Adelaide. As I reached for a handful of Valium I realised I'd just jumped into thin air protected by a rubber band. I laughed, and my fear of flying left me.

I have a photo of my father that I rarely look at. It's a well-composed black-and-white snap of him lying decapitated next to a log. It was taken, as a lark, with his mates, when he was perhaps twenty years old. One man lies with his head unseen behind a log with an axe on top, and Dad's disembodied head in rigor mortis lies to the other side of the log. This is eerily prescient of his violent death. But it was meant to be funny.

Death can be funny. At the opening of the Entertainment Centre in 1991, I ran into Con and Flo Polites. Dad had filmed George Polites' wedding, among other Polites family events.

Con Polites saw me and asked cheerily, 'How's your father?'

'Still dead,' I replied, and laughed.

Still dead.

The dead come to me in my dreams and I love that. They are still with me.

My father had shot countless hours of home movies of our family on Super 8 film, and lots of short subjects for his movie club, including a film about an old man visiting the grave of his lost love in the Barossa, as essayed by my grandfather Jos. There was also *The Tyro*, a film starring me, aged ten, as a kid being taught to surf at Cactus Beach. Happily, a stand-in was used for the actual surfing. This endless ribbon of dreams, this living, shadowy family history, was kept in boxes in my sister's cellar in Prospect until it was flooded and every single frame was ruined. Lost. Gone.

This loss was as bad as losing them from life. They'd gone again. Finally. They'd be taken from us and now their shadows had dissolved. Melted away.

So I'm left with the memory of a memory. A shot of my mother on a beach, demurring, then smiling, then walking along holding little Jenny's hand. They are happy and laughing, their blue eyes shining with love as they walk toward a bright, bright future.

Fade to black.

And then you forget everything but love. That's the really sad part of loss. After twenty-five or thirty years, you suddenly think, what did they smell like, what did they sound like, what did it feel like when they hugged you?

And you can't remember. But as absence becomes the only presence, you remember the love.

Jenny visited New Orleans the year after the tragedy and was given jewellery by the coroner, in two small buff-coloured envelopes marked with my parents' names and the numbers by which they were identified, and by which their remains were laid on a grid. Our father's watch is blackened by fire and the glass has gone. The hands of the watch are fused into the face of the watch at 4.09, the exact time of the crash. Jenny was given a charred chain, bangle and earrings retrieved from our mother's body, and her blackened watch which, incredibly, had kept going.

Coda

While writing this account, I was reminded by several people of something crucial that I'd forgotten, something I'd allowed the solace of time to erase. It was something shocking. I was the one who told my parents to go to New Orleans, probably because I was so enamoured by *A Streetcar Named Desire*. So they visited New Orleans and never left. I had also forgotten that I asked to go with them to New York, New Orleans and Las Vegas. But they denied me this and so I didn't die with them.

But I'm beyond guilt for this. I feel great guilt for being so preoccupied in my own life to have not even known that my parents, who lived in the next street, had left the country, that I never said goodbye. That I never thanked them or told them how much they meant to me, and how much I loved them. I hope they knew.

The remains of their bodies were found together and I hope they held hands in those last few seconds while they held on to life. I do know they loved to the end.

The cremated remains of Brian and Margaret Goers were

interred at Centennial Park Cemetery. Ellie bought the plot next to them and was buried there in 1992. Two years ago, the lease expired and we were required to pay $7500 for another twenty-five years. Both Jenny and I baulked at this, mainly because, should neither of us be extant in a quarter of a century's time, it's an unfortunate responsibility to hand to Jenny's children. So we paid to have the remains exhumed. I brought two headstones and three plastic boxes of ashes home. I talked to my parents and my grandmother all the long way home. Someday, sometime, somewhere, they will be given to the air of an afternoon almost past, but I can't yet let them fall again, even gently, to the earth.

The inscription on our parents' headstone quotes *A Streetcar Named Desire* and reads: 'Sometimes there's God so quickly.'

> *Sometimes, when I'm careless, I think survival is easy: you just keep moving forward with what you have, or what's left of what you were given, until something changes – or you realize, at last, that you can change without disappearing, that all you had to do was wait until the storm passes you over and you find that – yes – your name is still attached to a living thing.*

> Ocean Vuong, *On Earth We're Briefly Gorgeous*

Acknowledgements

I'm very thankful to my sister Jennifer White for her help with and support of this book, and of me, all our lives. This book has brought us closer together.

Kind thanks also to Robert Cusenza, Teresa Howie, Marie Edwards and Warren Jarrett for their memories and assistance, and to Julia Ledet and documentarian and writer Royd Anderson in New Orleans.

Thanks to the brilliant artist Richard Maurovic for permission to use his painting on the cover. Thanks also to Steven Raeburn who encouraged me to write deeper, and to the eagle-eyed early reader, the inestimable Valmai Hankel. And thanks to my friend and colleague and reader, Amy Verrall.

As ever, I'm eternally grateful to my dearest friend Samela Harris for her friendship, counsel and editorial acumen.

I love Wakefield Press, which generously puts my words between covers, and thanks to all there – a fine team. As an avid reader and habitué of all bookshops it is an abiding pleasure to see one's own work on the shelves. Wow!

Thanks especially to Michael Bollen, and the considerate and beautiful editor Julia Beaven. Any errors are mine.

Thanks to booksellers, librarians and, most of all, thanks to all readers.

My father thanks you, my mother thanks you, my sister thanks you and I thank you.

George M. Cohan's curtain-call sign-off.

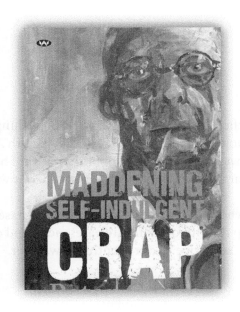

Peter Goers describes himself as 'a reformed social irritant'. A South Australian broadcaster, columnist, theatre guru and critic he has been known and loved for his sardonic wit and laconic flair for decades. This collection – which borrows its title from a review Goers once gave a Fringe show in the 80s, and now happily turns on himself – gathers the best of his Fringe shows, columns ('the very few I've taken a little pride in'), and a modicum of memoir. 'Like a bride's dress, these shows and this tome are something old, something new, something borrowed and something blue. Plus the nostalgic and the poignant,' he says.

This deliciously witty book features cameos from a who's who of the theatre and entertainment worlds, including anecdotes about Glenn Gould and Ethel Merman, friendships with Barry Humphries, Anne 'Willsy' Wills and Max Harris, close encounters with Angela Lansbury and Adriana Xenides, and fleeting moments with Tennessee Williams and Bette Davis.

For more information visit www.wakefieldpress.com.au

Wakefield Press is an independent publishing and
distribution company based in Adelaide, South Australia.
We love good stories and publish beautiful books.
To see our full range of books, please visit our website at
www.wakefieldpress.com.au
where all titles are available for purchase.
To keep up with our latest releases, news and events,
subscribe to our monthly newsletter.

Find us!

Facebook: www.facebook.com/wakefield.press
Twitter: www.twitter.com/wakefieldpress
Instagram: www.instagram.com/wakefieldpress